HOW TO PLAY

£2
ISBN

HOW TO PLAY

SOCCER

RONNIE GLAVIN

GUINNESS

Published by Guinness Books
33 London Road
Enfield
Middlesex EN2 6DJ

Produced and Designed by Mander Gooch Callow

Copyright © 1988 Mander Gooch Callow

Illustration: Sharon F. Gower

Printed and bound in Great Britain by
Hazell Watson & Viney Ltd., Aylesbury

British Library Cataloguing in Publication Data

    Glavin, Ronnie
      How to play soccer.
      1. Association Football – Manuals
      1. Title
      796.334'2

ISBN 0-85112-361-9

Contents

Introduction

Soccer is really a very basic game. The two main objectives are to score your own goals and prevent the opposition from scoring.

However, before you can begin to score goals or defend your area you must acquire some basic skills. The idea is to learn how to master the ball so that the movement of your body becomes fluid and you feel completely at ease when in possession of the ball.

Practice is the essence of all skill. Most people could keep a ball up in the air and kick reasonably well, but with practice at passing, kicking or any other skill you will become confident and proficient.

Everybody likes to have a kick about, but if you become capable with a ball you will enjoy displaying the control and tricks you have acquired with that practice.

Whether you learn control or tricks for fun or for a more serious approach to the game, you will appreciate when and how to use them in a game to enhance your performance.

After practice, experience is the next best thing for your game. Unfortunately neither of these qualities comes easily. No matter how long you have played or been involved in football there is always room for improvement or modification. If this was not true professional players would not train all week. They would relax for the week and only appear for a match on Saturday. As you know this does not happen and the whole idea is nonsense.

Professionals have to practise regularly at improving their skills and also at playing as a team. So as an individual it can only improve you as a player to learn how to pass, head, trap and dribble the ball.

Soccer is really no different from life. It is a constant process of learning. There is always someone who will be able to teach you something new or different. Every year I looked for ways to improve myself as a player and I am still learning now.

I hope my attitude and approach to the game will help you to become a better player. As I keep stressing nothing is easy, but if you keep an element of fun in your practice it can be infinitely more enjoyable.

Kit and Equipment

To play football there is only one piece of specialised equipment required – adequate footwear.

Boots

Boots must be comfortable and have sufficient grip to keep the wearer upright in the worst conditions, like thick mud. A particular type of boot may be the most expensive, but this does not mean it is the ideal answer for everyone. Cheaper boots may fit the bill just as well.

Comfort is very important and sometimes young people are ill-advised in sporting goods stores. Just because your favourite footballer wears a certain type of boot of expensive kangaroo leather, with screw-in studs this is not necessarily a recommendation to buy. These kind of gimmicks do not necessarily suit young needs.

Screw-in studs will cause blisters and much discomfort if used for example, on red shale pitches which predominate in Scotland.

Always go for comfort first and foremost when buying boots and although they are an expensive item, it is a mistake to buy boots a size too large to 'allow for growth'. Boots that are too large not only cause blisters, but you do not get the proper feel for the ball if your boots are too big and you cannot turn properly because of the effort needed to keep them on.

When wearing new boots for the first time many professionals smear the heel and top of the toe region with a liberal blob of Vaseline. This goes a long way towards helping to prevent blisters.

Caring for your boots
Always clean your boots after you have worn them. Scrape off all the excess mud with a flat-bladed knife. Then either scrub them or clean them with a cloth to remove all surface dirt. Stuff them with newspaper and allow them to dry naturally. Do not put them by the fire or radiator as this will crack the leather and mis-shape the boot.

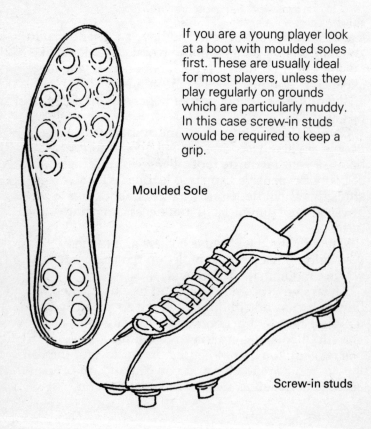

If you are a young player look at a boot with moulded soles first. These are usually ideal for most players, unless they play regularly on grounds which are particularly muddy. In this case screw-in studs would be required to keep a grip.

Moulded Sole

Screw-in studs

LAW-BREAKER

When you choose your boots bear in mind that you musn't wear anything which is dangerous to another player. The rules are very specific about this, for example :Bars must be made of leather or rubber and transverse and flat, not less than ½in wide. They must extend for the total width of the sole and be rounded at the corners.

Screw-in studs must be solid, replacable and made of leather, rubber, aluminium, plastic or similar material. The base mustn't stick out more than ¼ of an inch and the studs must be rounded, and not less that ½ in diameter.

Tapered studs must have a minimum diameter of ½ in. If the studs have a metal seating it must be embedded in the sole and any attachment screw must be part of the stud. There must be no other metal on the boot at all.

With moulded boots, studs must be made of rubber, plastic polyurethene or similar soft materials.

Provided that there are no fewer than ten studs on the sole, they must have a minimum diameter of 3/8 in.

THE REFEREE'S DECISION

If a player is found to be wearing boots or any other equipment which is dangerous to another player, he would be sent off to change. He would have wait until the ball was not in play and then report to the referee before coming-on again.

Once the boots are dry, put on a liberal coating of a good quality, wax shoe polish and leave the polish on until the next time they are needed. Then give the boots a good buffing. This should ensure that they stay looking good. But it is most important to clean them properly and thoroughly after each wearing and dry them naturally. They are the most expensive item of equipment you will buy, so give them the care they deserve.

Shin pads

The next most important item is shin pads. Young players usually show great reluctance when it comes to wearing them. But this should be overcome.

Try to wear pads in training and always when playing. Shin pads can now be bought in a very lightweight material, that is nowhere near as cumbersome as old-style pads. When you consider that these little items can prevent a broken leg or other serious injury then it is complete madness not to wear them.

None of the so-called 'hard' professional players would ever dare to venture out on to the pitch without shin pads and this should be a good enough example to follow.

The choice of most other items of kit is governed by the team or school side for which you play. The colour or design of shirts, shorts and socks will be chosen for you. But if possible buy natural fibres such as cotton. This is much better than nylon as cotton absorbs moisture and lets the skin breathe. Socks are available with cotton or lambswool feet and nylon leg sections. These are more expensive but help reduce problems such as blisters and fungal infections by reducing friction and sweating.

Fitness and Training

Fitness is a very important factor in any sport –
whether you are a professional or an amateur. The
level of fitness required depends on the standard at
which the chosen sport is to be played, for the love of
the game or at competition level.

Many people believe that a professional footballer's
fitness is not very different from their own. This could
not be further from the truth. Professionals train
intensively each day and reach a level of fitness which
is impossible for the average person to achieve without
the same effort and dedication.

Fitness is gauged by the amount of sustained effort
the body can endure. A professional may puff and
blow just as much as an amateur after a run, but the
difference is that the professional would be ready to
continue with further exertions for much longer.

An unfit person's heart can take a long time to
return to its normal rate of beating after exercise, but a
person who has worked at becoming fit will take
longer to increase his pulse rate and will need a shorter
time for it to return to normal.

Gauging your fitness
To gauge your fitness, take your pulse before a work-
out of any sort, then again straight after the exercise.
Time how long it takes for your pulse rate to return to
the first figure. This is an accurate guide to your

fitness. If you kept a record of these pulse rates you would see just how much more quickly you return to normal, the fitter you become. I shall elaborate further on endurance training and heart rates later on.

Today's game is played at a much higher tempo than it was 10 or 15 years ago. The degree of skill displayed by players has fallen during these years, but the increase in the level of fitness compensates for this decline.

I would recommend that any young players taking up football should work hard to improve their fitness level. This will enable them to play to a higher standard. Many people feel that there is no substitute for skill, but there should be a high fitness level too.

Skill alone will not make a professional player. Fitness is also needed. A fit player with mediocre skills can make the professional ranks.

If you were to give ex-professional players a ball, most can still display admirable skills, probably more so than their counterpart's today. But try and compare fitness levels and there IS no comparison.

Today's players are much fitter and have a more professional attitude than those of yesteryear. A well-worn professional saying is that if you train easily the games are hard, if you train hard the games are easy. This is definitely true!

Team Fitness

These days many professional teams do a considerable amount of long distance running as part of their pre-season build-up. This can be as much as 8 to 10 miles a day, not including any work before or after the run. It is felt that this builds up stamina. I shall cover stamina training at greater length later.

Things have changed considerably since I first started playing for a professional club in 1968. The attitude to fitness then was a bit of a joke. I remember reporting back for pre-season training after a 2 month summer break and a number of players had gained a great deal of weight – anything up to 20 lbs. It was a grand event, being weighed in front of all the team, seeing who had the largest gain and suffering the barrage of personal abuse. Then trying to get fit again with the extra weight, extra clothes and plastic sweat-suits to lose the weight, would make every mile of running seem like 20.

This just would not happen today. There is no great weigh-in. Players are just too professional now to allow themselves to lose their fitness in two months.

Young players are more conscious today of their own health and fitness. There is no easy way to get fit, but better facilities make it much more enjoyable. A good gym instructor will advise on a programme of exercises to suit your particular needs.

Getting fit

The aspects of fitness which need to be developed are gauged differently according to which sport you play.

I recall a professional sprinter coming along to join in training with one of the teams I played for. His methods of training were totally different from those of the professional footballer.

We held a race, which was to be over 100 yards. The sprinter left every one of the players standing after 40 yards. Over a straight distance race, with a start off and build up of speed, he won hands down. However football players work on exercises called 'shuttles' and 'doggies'. These concentrate on short sharp runs of about 10 to 20 yards. You set off, flat out, towards a marker, turn and race back. The sprinter was only mediocre at this exercise, with many players beating him. It is not very often a player is required to do a 100 yard sprint in a game, but he will be called upon many times to run, flat out, for 5 to 10 yards. If he is sharp

over this short distance, it can make all the difference
to his getting the ball or losing it to a faster opponent.
Probably the longest sprint required of a player would
be about 60 yards, so the football player has to be more
versatile, sharp at the short runs, yet able to do more
distance if required.

There is no chance of building up your speed over 5
yards, the burst has to be almost instantaneous, so
players work hard on these short runs, as well as their
longer sprints.

Weight training

I must add a few notes about weight training. Weights
are invaluable to football players to maintain a good
shape and help build muscle after injury, but they
MUST be used properly. Never lift heavy weights.
Weightlifters do not make football players. The use of
heavy weights has an adverse effect on your running.
Use light weights and do more repetitions (or reps), do
not be tempted to increase the weight. Young players
must get advice if they are really serious about using
weights. A good gym instructor should be able to help.

I would like to add a short note on the development
of young players with particular regard to their skill
and fitness. I cannot stress enough that young players
should not go on long runs or do any other type of
stamina building work. This is totally unnecessary.

Youngsters have natural stamina and do not need
this type of training until their bodies have stopped
growing. If you are a young player you should
concentrate on the development of skills.

An ideal programme would consist of ball control,
heading, dribbling, passing and shooting. All
incorporated into short games which are fun yet
competitive.

I have illustrated this by giving an example of the
development of young players by age and showing
roughly what a training programme should consist of.

Age 6 – 8: The aim is fun. The rules should be made up by the players themselves. Use a soft ball (size 3) and small goals. Best games are four-a-side inside a 40 x 30 yard pitch.

Age 8 – 10: The aim is fun, introducing skills. The rules should be slightly modified to resemble the rules of the 'big' game. Keep using the soft ball and small goals. Increase the size of teams from four to six and the pitch to a larger size of 60 x 40 yards.

Age 10 – 12: This is when you pick up most skills, so concentrate on developing them. Use the rules you are used to and work within that framework. Start using a larger, harder ball (size 4). The games should now be seven against seven with the pitch enlarged to 70 x 50 yards.

Age 12 – 14: Keep working on the skills and start to bring in tactical ideas and awareness. The individual needs to learn what is wanted within this new, more sophisticated framework. The rules should now be those used in professional football. The ball, pitch and goals should be standard. The sides can be either full eleven or eight.

Age 14 – 16: Keep on with the basics, but take the tactical side a step further. This is the time to start work on fitness.

Age 16 – 18: Now is the time to cope with problems that will arise, caused by playing the full game. Learning by mistakes is better at this stage. Work can also begin on specialised training, moves and positional play.

Flexibility

Whatever your sport and whatever your reasons are for doing that sport, it is very, very important to stretch your muscles before the slightest exertion. It is so easy to pull a cold, tight muscle. Stretching serves to warm up the body by increasing the blood flow to the muscles and joint areas. Naturally this will improve athletic performance and also lessen the risk of injury. More attention should be focused on making the body flexible during training.

Flexibility is an absolute must for a competitive sportsman. A short but intense stretching routine will be invaluable in body flexibility.

One of the main reasons that an athlete should stretch, is that the more flexible he is, the faster he can run. Since nearly all athletic events require speed, all athletes should work to become as flexible as possible. Another very important reason is that a flexible football player is much less susceptible to a variety of injuries. Prevention of such damage is much better than cure. Muscular injuries are notoriously difficult to cure, taking weeks and sometimes months of treatment.

The stretching programme outlined here is designed to stretch the large muscles throughout the body and increase the range of motion in major joint areas. It is vital to stress that flexibility should encompass the whole body.

You should start to stretch gently until you reach a point where there is a resistance, then ease off slightly. After holding this position for 30 seconds, move to a point where resistance is felt again, hold on for 30 seconds then relax.

There should never be any discomfort. If pain is felt during stretching then there is a real risk of injury. It should be done in a slow, relaxed fashion.

Steady, deep breathing should be maintained at all times. Do not hold your breath. The deep breathing will keep you relaxed and it is important to be in that state while carrying out your programme.

Bouncing when stretching is unnecessary and downright dangerous. The 'bounce' eventually forces the muscle to tighten in an effort to protect itself, so eventually this forced motion results in muscular injury.

Stretching is not a competitive exercise. Each person has his own level of flexibility. What one person can do easily, another may find too difficult to achieve. Therefore two players can never be compared in terms of flexibility. Each should realise that stretching is for self-improvement and players should always strive to improve their own ability in whatever way they can.

As with skill, flexibility comes with time and consistent effort. You will also become aware of which parts of your body need the most work. For instance, you may have very flexible thighs which require only a little stretching, whereas your upper shoulders and arms may be really stiff and require extra time and work. Keep in tune with your own body because it will let you know your individual requirements.

FAULT-FINDER

The correct technique for stretching exercises uses a smooth gradual motion. There should be no jerks whatsoever.

The Stretches

1. Calf stretch

Face a wall, stand a little distance from it, and rest your forearms on it for support, with your forehead on the back of your hands.

Now bend one knee and bring it towards the support. Your back leg should be straight with your foot flat and pointed straight ahead or slightly toe-in.

Now, without changing the position of your feet, slowly move your hips forward, as you keep your back leg straight and your foot flat. Create an easy feeling of stretch in your calf muscle. Hold an easy stretch for 20 seconds, then increase the stretch, feeling very slightly into a developmental stretch for 20 seconds.

Don't overstretch. Now, switch legs.

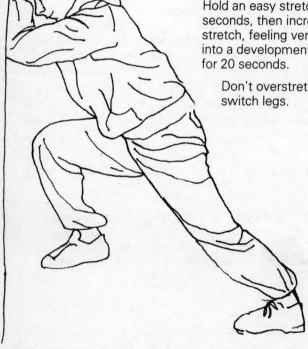

2. Sitting groin stretch

Sit on the floor, with the soles of your feet together. Your hands should be around your feet and toes. Be sure to keep your heels a comfortable distance from your crotch. Now gently pull your upper body forward until you feel an easy stretch in your groin area. Hold an easy stretch for 20 seconds. If you are doing it correctly, it will feel good; the longer you hold the stretch, the less you should feel it.

Do not initiate the movement forward from your head and shoulders. This will round your shoulders and put pressure on your lower back. Be sure to concentrate on making the initial move forward from your hips. Keep your lower back flat.

After you feel the tension diminish slightly, increase the stretch, by gently pulling yourself a little further into it. Now it should feel a bit more intense but not painful. Hold this for about 25 seconds.

3. Hamstring stretch

Next, straighten your right leg as you keep your left leg bent. The sole of your left foot should be facing the inside of your right upper leg. Now, bend forward FROM YOUR HIPS until the slightest, easiest feeling of stretch is created. Hold this for 30 seconds. Be sure to initiate the stretch from your hips. Keep your chin in a neutral position. Be sure that the foot of the leg being stretched is upright with your ankle and toes relaxed.

After the feeling of the easy stretch has subsided, slowly go into the developmental stretch for 20-30 seconds. Do not worry about how far you can go. A very slight distance may be all that is needed.

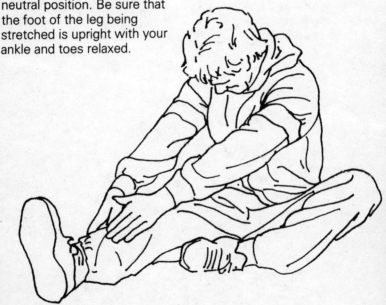

4. Sitting groin stretch
Repeat previous stretch.

5. Lying groin stretch

Now lie on your back with the soles of your feet together. Let your knees fall apart. Relax your hips as you let gravity give you a very mild stretch in your groin area. Stay in this very relaxed position for 40 seconds. Really concentrate on letting go of any tension, do not force anything. The stretch feeling will be subtle and should happen naturally.

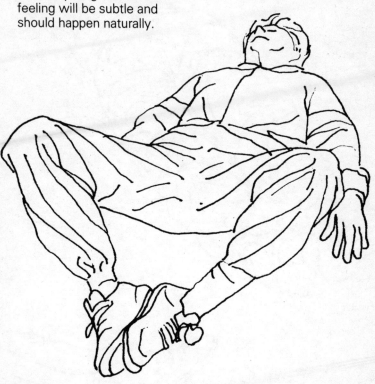

6. Straight body stretch

Slowly straighten both legs. With your arms overhead, reach with your arms and hands while you point your toes. This is an elongation stretch. Hold a controlled, good stretch for 5 seconds, then relax. Repeat 3 times.

Each time you stretch, gently pull in your abdominal muscles to make the middle of your body thin.

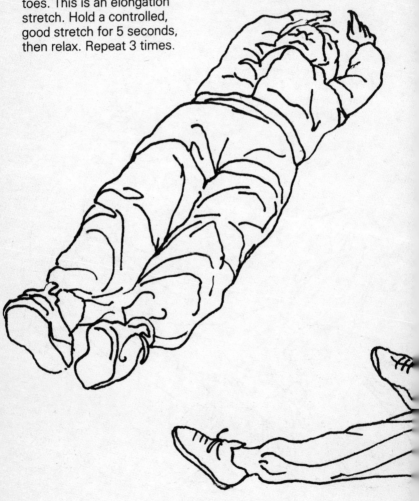

7. Lower back stretch

Next, bend one knee and
gently pull it towards your
chest, until you feel an easy
stretch. Hold for 40 seconds.
You may feel a stretch in
your lower back; if you do
not, do not worry about it.
Repeat with the other leg.

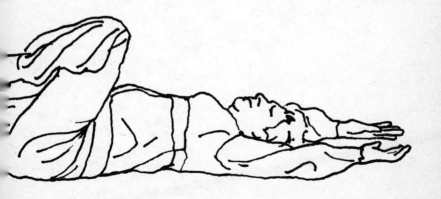

8. Neck stretch

Next, with both knees bent,
feet flat on the floor, interlace
your fingers behind your
head at about ear level. Now,
use the power of your arms
to slowly pull your head
forwards until you feel a
slight stretch in the back of
your neck. Hold for 5-10
seconds, then slowly return
to the starting position.
Do this 3 or 4 times.

9. Shoulder blade pinch

Pull your shoulder blades together to create tension in your upper back. Hold this controlled tension for 4-5 seconds, then relax and gently pull your head forwards as in the previous stretch.
Repeat both 3 or 4 times.

10. Hip and hamstring stretch

Sit up, straighten one leg and bend the other knee. Set the bent leg on top of the straight leg with the ankle of the bent leg, resting just to the outside of the other leg and just above (not on) your knee. Now gently bend forward from your hips, until an easy tension is felt behind your knee and hold for 20 seconds. Hold the developmental stretch for 15 seconds. Try to keep your bent knee close to the ground.

11. Quadriceps stretch

Lie on your left side and rest the side of your head in the palm of your left hand. Hold the top of your right foot with your right hand, between the toes and ankle joint. Gently pull the right heel toward the right buttock to stretch the ankle and quadriceps.
Hold an easy stretch for 10 seconds.
NEVER STRETCH THE KNEE TO THE POINT OF PAIN.

12. Shoulder stretch 1

With arms extended overhead and palms together, stretch arms upwards and slightly backwards. Breathe in as you stretch upwards, holding the stretch for 5-8 seconds.

13. Shoulder stretch 2

To stretch your shoulder and the middle of your upper back, gently pull your elbow across your chest towards your opposite shoulder. Hold for 10 seconds.

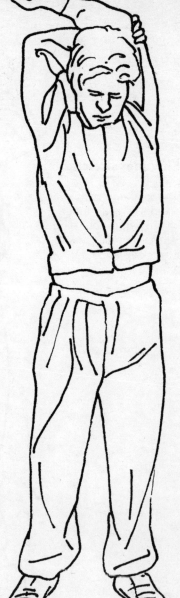

14. Shoulder stretch 3

With your arms overhead, hold the elbow of one arm with the hand of the other arm. Gently pull the elbow behind your head slowly, holding the stretch for 15 seconds.

Endurance Training

Football is a game of running and endurance. This is true whichever position you play in – unless it is goalkeeper.

Running, in relation to endurance training, deals with the heart. Like other muscles in the body the heart can be strengthened by 'over-loading'. It cannot, however, become any larger, as other muscles can. To achieve this level of over-loading, the heart beat rate has to be raised and maintained at this higher rate, over a prolonged period. Short bursts of speed such as sprint training will not produce these prolonged high heartbeat rates because of the short period of effort involved. This does not mean that sprint training is unnecessary. It is very useful, but it is different to endurance training in many crucial ways.

A stronger heart will be able to pump blood to the muscles faster. This in turn results in oxygen being delivered to fuel the working muscles and waste products being eliminated from them more quickly.

Endurance training – also called cardiovascular training – is at its most effective when it involves three phases. These are: long distance, jog and stride and 'interval training'. This type of programme ensures that players will be prepared to play as well in the closing stages of a game as they did at the beginning.

Remember that the following programme is for endurance training and not for speed.

Long distance phase
This is the first stage of the programme, requiring distances of two to three miles to be covered three to four days a week.

The best way to condition yourself aerobically for these distances is to monitor your heart rate. It also happens that this is the easiest and least painful way of running distances. This sounds complicated and will probably require a pen and paper and some effort to determine your particular rate figures. The effort is worth it and once you have worked out your own personal figures your training will fall into place and become straightforward.

To determine your heart rate:

1. Subtract your age from 220 (this is the maximum allowable heart rate). Let's take an example age of 16. Therefore the figure is 204.

2. Multiply this figure by 70%. The figure become 143. This is the lower limit of the exercise heart rate.

3. Multiply the figure in (1) by 80%. this is 163 and that represents the upper limit for the heart rate.

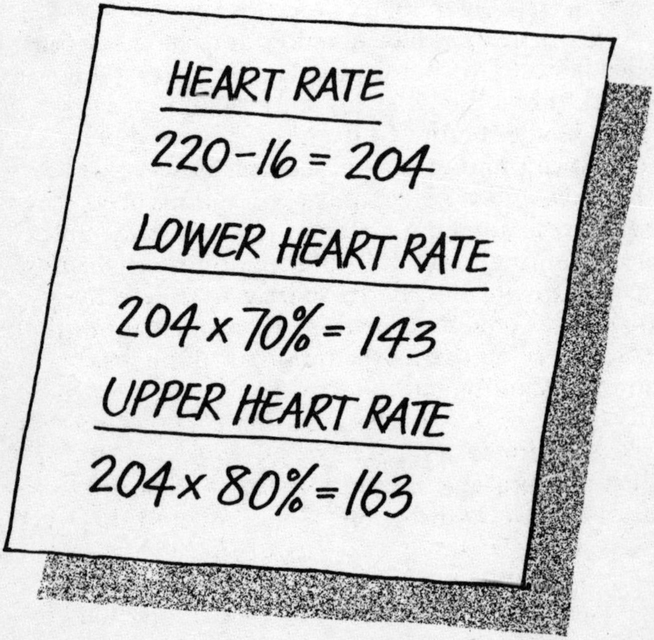

HEART RATE

$$220 - 16 = 204$$

LOWER HEART RATE

$$204 \times 70\% = 143$$

UPPER HEART RATE

$$204 \times 80\% = 163$$

So a 16 year-old should run at a pace to keep his heart rate between 143 and 163. Stop occasionally and take a 10 second pulse count. Work out beforehand what yours should be. A 16 year-old should have about 25 beats per 10 seconds, working out at 150 per minute, which is a figure halfway between the limits. You can adjust your pace as required. If the beats are over the upper limit then slow down. If they are under the lower limit, speed up.

When you have done all this technical work, merely run at this pace for 20 to 25 minutes, three or four days a week and your aerobic or heart conditioning will improve substantially. This stamina is the difference between winning or losing games. If you are as fresh at the end of a match as you are at the start, you will hopefully have the advantage over your opponent. At least he will not have one over you.

This long distance training should be done on alternate days. It should be done on a soft surface to prevent any injuries to the shins or feet. This should cover the first four weeks of the programme.

Jog and stride phase
This second phase requires alternate jogging and striding over a long distance without a rest period. This type of training is done over two to three miles, the player jogging for 200 yards followed by striding for 200 yards. Striding is the pace in between the jog and sprint. The important part of this training is that there is no rest period over the entire distance. So the sequence is jog 200 yards, stride 200 yards, jog 200 yards, stride 200 yards, etc. This prepares the player for intense efforts after shorter recovery periods. He begins to train through the pain threshold and develop mental toughness.

Interval training phase

This third phase of the programme is speed work at a given pace with timed rest periods.

The distance the player is required to run should be between 120 and 200 yards with a rest period of between 30 and 90 seconds.

The reason for distances of 120 and 200 yards is that some emphasis can be given now to running. The heart rate can still be driven up to its training rate.

Here the rest period is of equal importance. Anything less than 30 seconds does not allow sufficient time for the heart to refill with blood. Yet anything over 90 seconds is too long as the heart rate starts to drop below a level that will gain anything from the endurance.

Once again this is not a speed programme, but one for endurance, to ensure that the player is as competitive late in the game, as he is in the opening stages.

Passing and Trapping

Once you have improved your fitness, you can begin
to concentrate on improving your skills

One of the elementary skills in football is passing the
ball. There are various different types of pass. They
consist of the instep pass, lofted instep pass, inside
and outside of the foot pass, swerving pass and the
volley.

There are three main points to keep in mind when
passing the ball. The first is positioning; considering
the position of your body when striking the ball. If
your posture is wrong when making the pass, the ball
could go well away from where you intended it to
land.

Accuracy is the second point. How accurately you
line yourself up to strike the ball and which part of the
ball you hit are both vital factors. The third point is
concentration. As with every other ball game, the most
important part of concentration is always to keep your
eye on the ball. It will also help if you can concentrate
and think ahead about what you will do with the ball
before you even gain control of it.

Passing

Keeping these points in mind you can learn to execute the passes mentioned previously.

All passing starts with the same approach.

As you near the ball, position your non-striking foot alongside it. This foot should be pointing in the direction you wish the ball to travel. The accuracy factor will be determined by the path and speed of your pass. This will dictate where and how hard you strike the ball. Before you hit the ball make sure your intended path is clear of opponents. After checking this, concentrate on keeping your eyes on the ball.

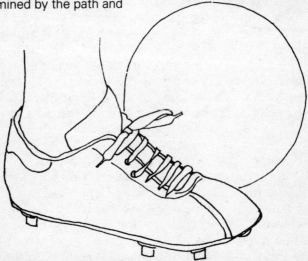

As with any soccer skills there are many decisions you must make in a split second when passing. How hard must I hit the ball? Which part of the foot shall I use? Where do I want the ball to go? This sounds like an impossible task to do so quickly, but remember that with practice, practice and more practice it will become quite easy.

Instep pass

The instep of the foot is the
shoelace area from the top of
the ankle to the top of the
toes.
This kick is mainly used for
long distance passes and fast
shots at goal. It is the most
widely used pass and will
probably account for more
than 80% of the passes you
will make in the game.
With toes pointed down, the
kick should come from the
knee and NOT the hip. You
are using your calf muscle to
obtain the power.

The knee of your kicking foot should be bent over the ball. Tighten the muscles in your kicking foot just before you strike the ball. You are aiming to hit the centre of the ball and your foot and leg must follow through in a flowing movement, in the direction that you wish the ball to go.

As most instep kicks are used for long low passes you will find that if you lean forward while kicking the ball it will stay nearer the ground.

Since this is the most frequently used pass you should practise it often – and also with both feet – to improve your skill. Using both feet will make a much more versatile player.

Lofted instep pass

The lofted instep pass uses the same part of the foot as the ordinary instep pass. This kick is used when you want the ball to rise up in the air, over an opponent, to a team-mate.

The pass is performed in exactly the same way as the instep pass, except that instead of keeping your body over the ball to keep the pass low, the reverse is true. You lean backwards and strike beneath the ball, not in the centre. These two changes will give you the lift you require to place the ball over your opponent.

The lofted instep pass is used mostly for corner kicks or wingers, crossing the ball into the area.

Inside of the foot pass

The inside of the foot is the area from your heel to your big toe. This area of the foot is used for shorter passes of, say, up to 20 yards and also when dribbling the ball. This is the easiest of the passes because such a large area of the foot is used.

As usual, position your non-kicking foot in the direction you wish the ball to go. Raise your kicking foot 2-3 inches off the ground, so that you will hit the centre of the ball with your kick. Bring your foot back and strike firmly through the centre, letting your foot follow through, to guide the ball in the proper direction. This pass comes from the hip using the thigh muscle for power.

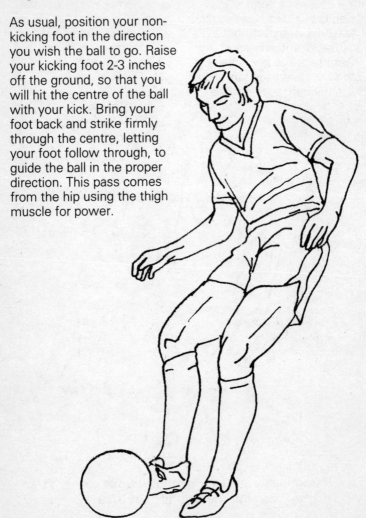

Outside of the foot pass

The outside of the foot is the flat area from the ankle to the end of the toes. This pass is used for short, quick passes, dribbling or shots at goal. It is mainly used by more skilful experienced players, but as with any skill it can be learned with proper practice.

The knee and the kicking foot are turned inwards and the outside front of the foot is used to make contact with the ball. Raise the foot slightly off the ground and aim to strike the centre of the ball.

Swerving pass

This is a trick pass and uses either the inside or the outside of the foot. It can literally swerve the ball in a curved path rather than a straight one.

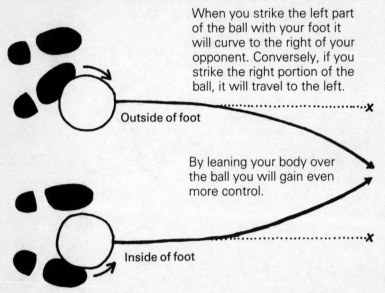

When you strike the left part of the ball with your foot it will curve to the right of your opponent. Conversely, if you strike the right portion of the ball, it will travel to the left.

Outside of foot

By leaning your body over the ball you will gain even more control.

Inside of foot

The uses of this pass are fairly obvious, like swerving the ball round a wall or for an inswinging corner.

FAULT-FINDER

Remember to keep your non-kicking foot alongside the ball. It is used only for balance apart from pointing in the direction of the pass. Most of your weight should be on your kicking foot as it hits the ball.

Volley

The full volley is really more of a shot than a pass. It is particularly effective for shots on goal as the ball is travelling fast and with considerable power. To give this power, the instep part of the foot is used in the full volley.

Concentration is vital to this kick if you do not want to punch fresh air. Watch the ball closely as it comes towards you. At the right moment when the ball is 12-16 inches in the air, balance on your non-kicking leg, raise the kicking foot to meet the ball as it falls. The toe should be pointed down as you make contact to give maximum power.

FAULT-FINDER

Be careful when using either volley to avoid being penalised for dangerous kicking. This is a foul when the kicking leg is above waist-level, while other players are close by.

Half-volley

The half-volley uses all the same basics as the full volley, except that you strike the ball after it bounces once on the ground. This pass demands full concentration because you want to make contact with the ball no more than a few inches up from its point of bounce.

As it is rising, swing your leg from the side and strike the ball with your instep. Try to follow your kick through as this will give the ball more speed and power. It must be said that it is not as powerful as the full volley, but can cause a goalkeeper a lot of problems when used correctly.

LAW-BREAKER

Never let your enthusiasm for or frustration with the game get the better of you. The referee can penalize you for misconduct or ungentlemanly behaviour and if you carry on, suspend you from the game.
You will be sent off for violent conduct, serious foul play or the use of foul or abusive language.

Trapping

Trapping – or the control and stopping of the ball – is a basic skill and the first ingredient in making the ball do what you want it to do. You must gain control before you make a pass, dribble or make a shot on goal.

All traps share the main objective, stopping the ball within a foot of your body. When you have done this and gained control you are ready to take off again.

To trap the ball effectively, you must keep in mind the same three main points that you use for passing. To recap, these are positioning, accuracy and concentration.

Positioning
– Get your body close to the ball. Go out and meet the ball, do not hang back waiting.
Accuracy
- Which part of the body will you use to trap the ball?
Concentration
– It must be stressed how important it is to keep your eye on the ball in flight as it approaches you. A momentary lapse can make everything go wrong.

There are six main traps which are commonly used. These are the sole, inside and outside of the foot, instep, thigh and chest traps.

FAULT-FINDER

Keep your balance on your standing leg and remember not to slam your trapping foot down on top of the ball. This can cause your trapping foot to roll off the ball and then you will fall over.

Sole trap

This is one of the most basic and simple traps. The bottom of your foot, from the ball of your foot to your heel, is used for this trap. This is quite a large area, which makes it easier for you. It is used mainly when a player has to reach out with his leg to trap the ball.

First of all, as with the passes, position yourself correctly and be ready to receive the ball and trap it. You should know already that the ball is going to land at your feet or that you are going to want it as it bounces. As the ball approaches, you should begin to lift your leg, bending it from the knee. You should be directly in the flight path of the ball, concentrating on where it will land. As the ball begins to drop, about level with your knee, be ready to bring your foot down on the ball as it touches the ground.

Your sole should be directly over as it touches the ground. If it is not the ball can run away from under your foot.

Inside of the foot trap

This is also a relatively easy trap because of the large area of your foot used. This area is from the heel to the big toe, on the inside of your foot. This trap is used for a ball that is travelling towards you hard and fast, or to control a ground level pass from a team-mate.

Once again as the ball is approaching you make sure that you are positioned correctly. Your trapping foot should be turned outwards and raised slightly off the ground ready to meet the ball. As the ball hits the inside of your foot, relax it and allow it to withdraw backwards slightly, to absorb the impact like a cushion. If you do this correctly the ball will stop dead.

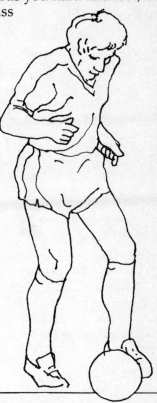

FAULT-FINDER

If you hold your foot and leg too stiffly and are rigid the ball will bounce off your foot. Practise letting your foot relax. Your body and the ball will be in harmony eventually.

Outside of the foot trap
This is probably the most difficult of the traps to
master, but again with practice you can become
proficient enough to use this trap in your game. It is
usually used to control and settle bouncing balls that
arrive by your side.

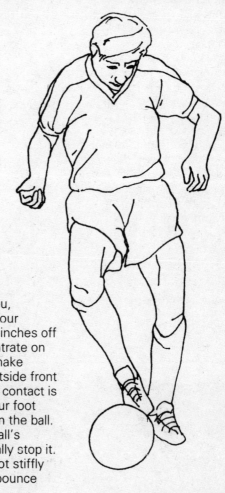

As the ball nears you,
prepare by raising your
trapping foot a few inches off
the ground. Concentrate on
getting the ball to make
contact with the outside front
of your boot. When contact is
made, withdraw your foot
inwards and cushion the ball.
This will slow the ball's
motion and eventually stop it.
Do not hold your foot stiffly
or the ball will just bounce
away from you.

Instep trap

The instep of the foot or lace area trap is used for high dropping balls. It is another difficult trap to master, simply because the area used is much smaller than the inside or outside of the foot. Even many professionals find this trap difficult. Good practice for this trap is to juggle the ball from foot to foot and try to balance the ball on your instep. This is one skill you can practise endlessly on your own too.

The method for this trap is very similar to that of the sole trap.

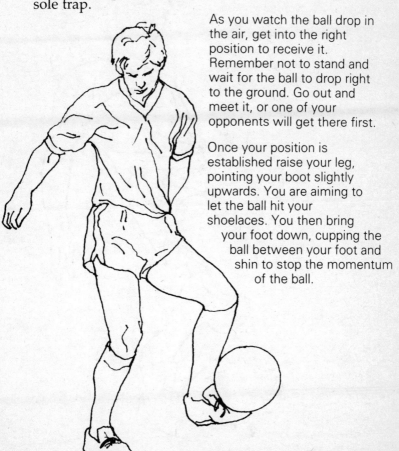

As you watch the ball drop in the air, get into the right position to receive it. Remember not to stand and wait for the ball to drop right to the ground. Go out and meet it, or one of your opponents will get there first.

Once your position is established raise your leg, pointing your boot slightly upwards. You are aiming to let the ball hit your shoelaces. You then bring your foot down, cupping the ball between your foot and shin to stop the momentum of the ball.

Thigh Trap

This trap, like the instep trap, is used for controlling dropping balls. You use the top area of your thigh between groin and knee.

While the ball is falling, lift your thigh up to meet the ball. Lean back slightly, using your standing leg and arms for balance. As the ball hits your thigh, withdraw the leg slightly downwards to cushion the ball. This will stop the ball, and then you simply straighten your leg, allowing the ball to drop neatly to your feet.

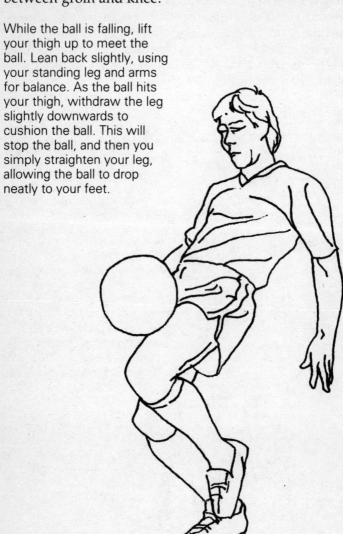

Chest trap

The chest and thigh traps are much simpler to carry out than, for example the instep trap, because you are using a larger area of your body to control the ball. The chest trap is used when a ball is coming too high or too close for a foot trap.

In preparation you should arch your back as the ball approaches. Thrust your chest out a little as the ball makes contact, again forming a cushion against the impact. After the ball hits your chest relax it and the ball will drop to your feet ready for you to make the next move.

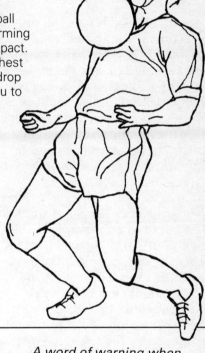

FAULT-FINDER

A word of warning when using the chest trap in a proper game: keep your arms and hands spread wide to avoid being penalised by the referee for hand ball.

Ball Control

As with any skill, you will only become proficient at ball control with practice. Most people can become reasonably good at ball control, but it takes real effort and repeated practice to make this their strong point.

Many professionals today would list ball control as their weak point, but credit must be given to those players, as they have worked hard to bring their weakest link up to an adequate standard.

Whichever aspect of your game is weak, or even downright poor, you can still work and strengthen it to a more acceptable level.

A perfect example of a recent-day player who did this was Kevin Keegan. I think if there is anyone to look up to as an example in football, including the most skilful of footballers, it is K.K. If a poll were to be taken, asking people involved in professional football, to list the 'top ten' players in Britain in the last ten years who they consider to be most skilful, Kevin Keegan would probably not figure in any list. But ask the same people to list the 'top ten' world class players produced by Britain in the last 10 years, and he would probably be in everyone's top three. This illustrates how a player can recognise his limitations and work hard to overcome them. A skilful player is not necessarily going to be a world class player, but conversely a player who has no outstanding skills can become a great player. That is the way the game is played.

So how do you acquire those skills? Well, it is significant that the Dutch methods of dribbling and mastering ball control are being adopted by the English FA at their school of excellence. This is the way that the cream of young players are being taught to develop their skills.

It certainly works for the Dutch. They have shown that you do not have to be a brilliant player to be comfortable with the ball. Ruud Gullit is not the only Dutch player who can control and pass the ball and display all the world-class skills that the experts talk about. Even their defenders can play and make good use of the ball. If you model yourself on the Dutch players you will be able to adapt your game and play in most positions. That is the key to their philosophy of total football.

LAW-BREAKER
The ball is out of play when it has wholly crossed the goal-line, whether on the ground or in the air, and when the game has been stopped by the Referee. The ball is in play at all other times from the start of the match to the finish including when it rebounds from a goal-post, cross-bar or corner-flag post into the field of play. If it rebounds off either the Referee or Linesmen when they are in the field of play and in the event of a supposed infringement of the Laws, until a decision is given.

Dribbling

The following drills are a brief resumé of those used by the Dutch. If you use them in your practice they will be an invaluable aid to improving your game and skill level:

1. Dribbling the ball with the inside and outside of the foot.

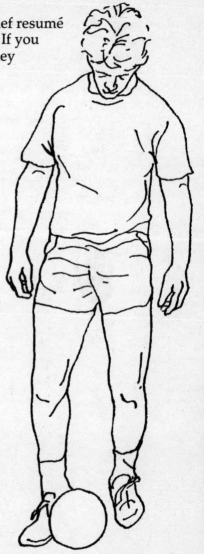

Try the movement with both
left and right feet.

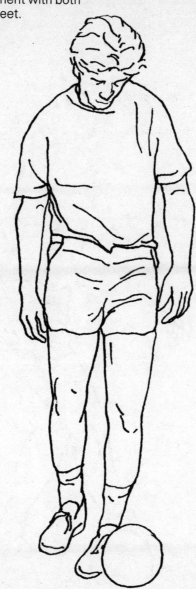

2. Turning with the outside of
the foot.

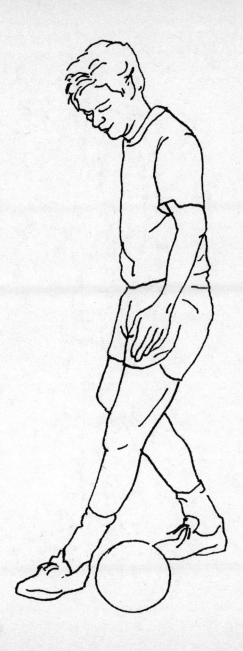

3. Turning using the inside of
the foot and driving away
using the outside of the foot.

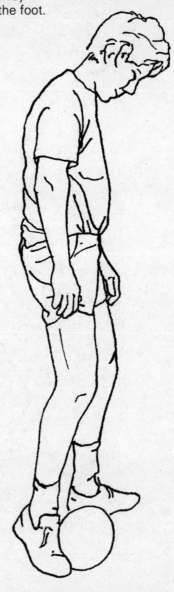

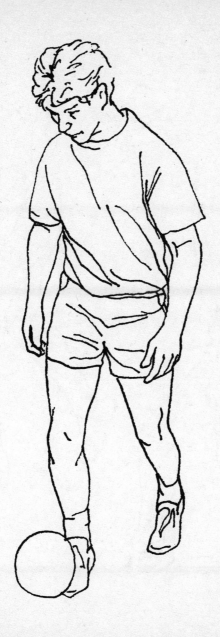

4. Throw the leg over the ball
and turn. Taking it away with
the inside of the foot.

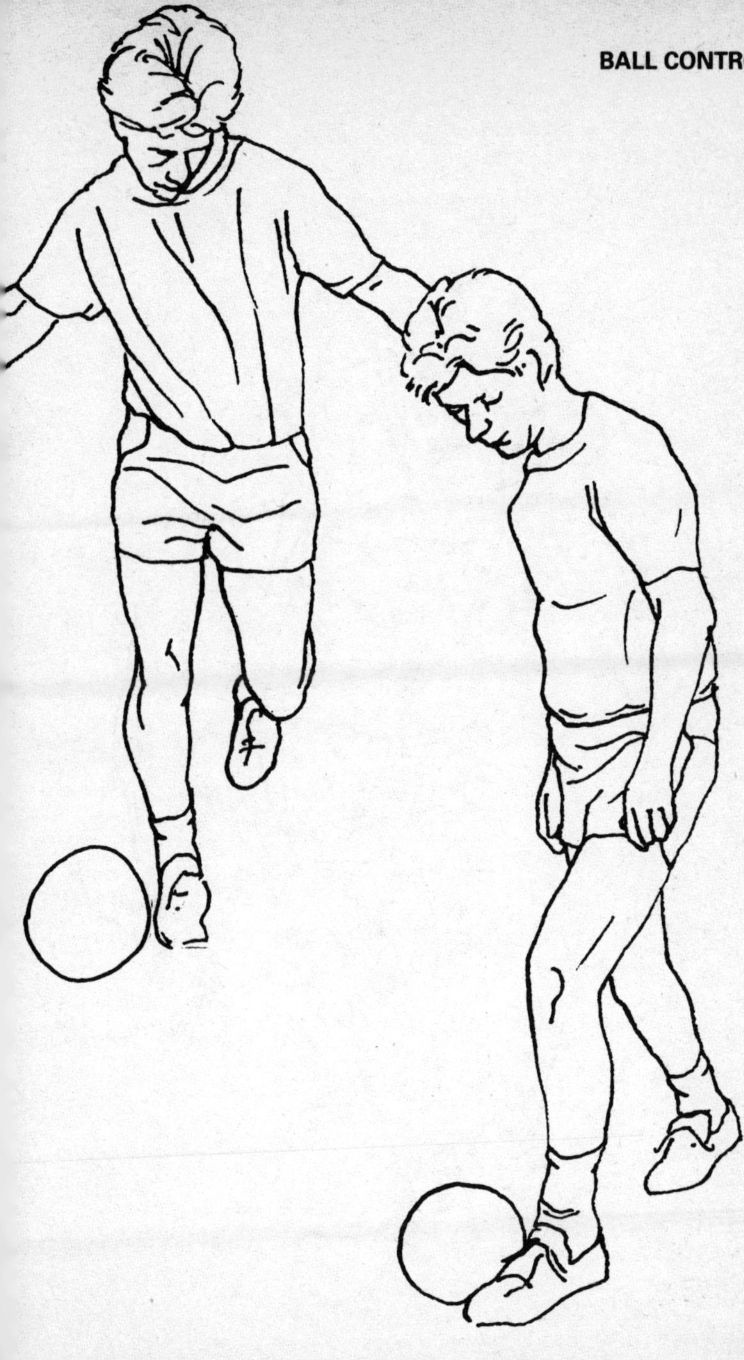

5. Stop the ball behind you
and drive away using the
outside of the foot.

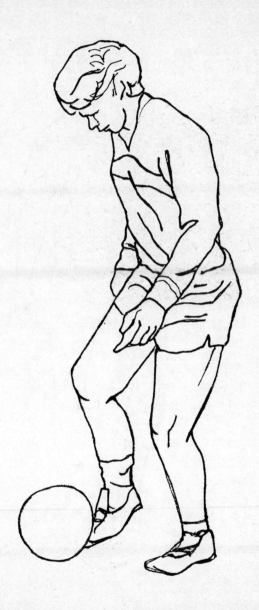

6. Using the sole of the foot
drag the ball across the body
and then drive away with the
outside of the foot.

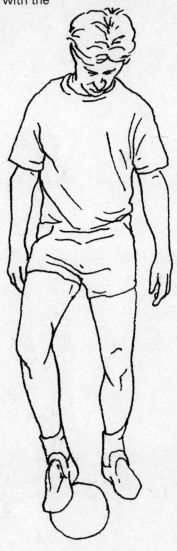

7. Stop the ball with the inside of the foot on top of the ball, then drag the ball across the body.

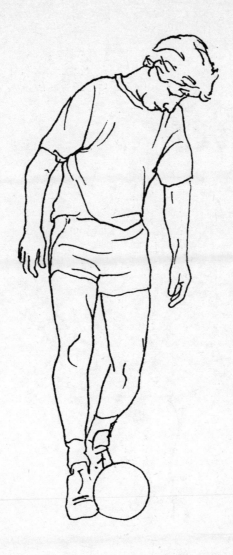

8. Stop the ball, go past it
and drive away using the
outside of the foot.

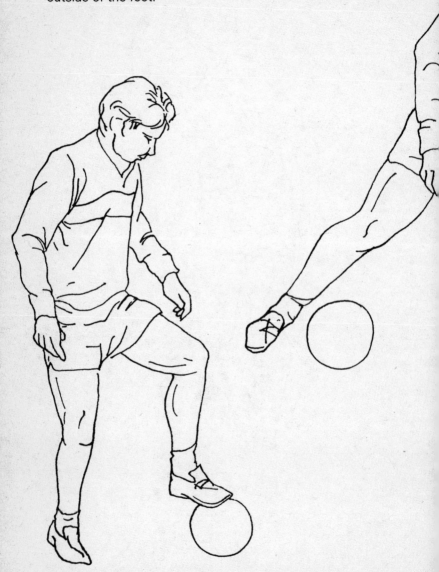

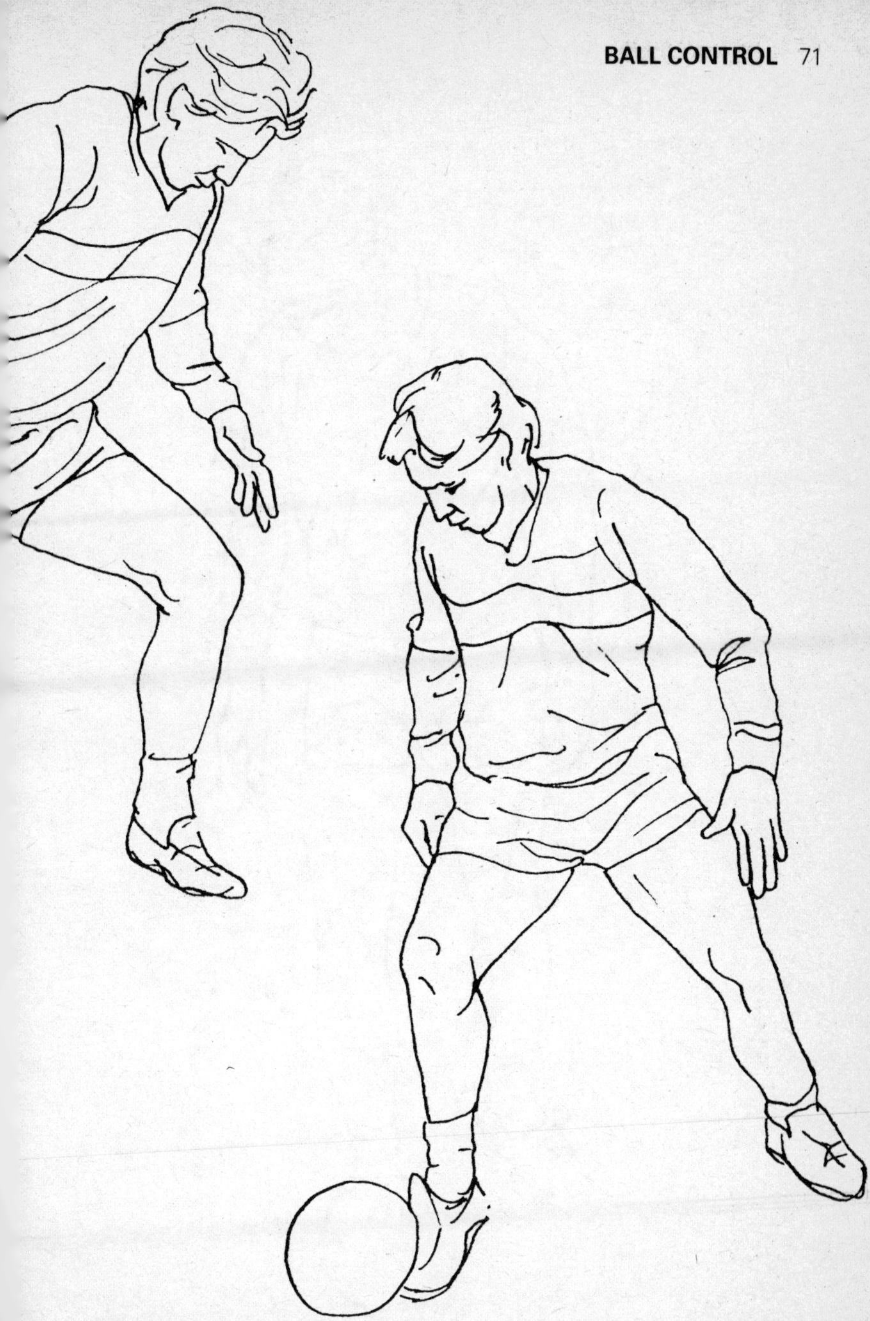

9. Play the ball with the inside of either foot and throw a leg over the ball.

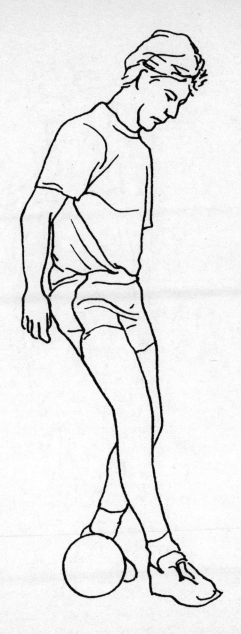

10. Stop the ball, drag it back
with the sole of the foot.

Push away using the outside
of the foot.

11. The Johann Cruyff trick.
Stop the ball. Position
yourself above the ball, then
flick it, with the inside of the
foot, between your legs and
away from your opponent.

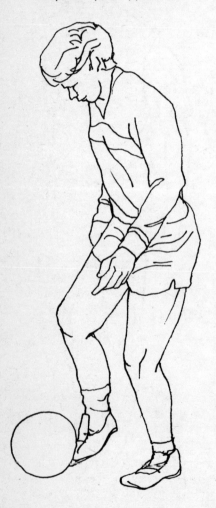

If you practise these drills regularly, together with the trapping and passing techniques in the previous chapter, you will have good all round skills which will be useful in whatever position you play.

Heading

The technique of heading uses the area between the hairline and eyebrows (the forehead) to hit the ball in a certain direction.

When you prepare to head the ball you must firstly position yourself properly to meet the ball. The next two points are those which are common to every skill: concentration and accuracy.

Concentrate on the ball, always keep your eyes on it, then think about where you want the ball to go. The accuracy of your header depends on your jumping to meet the ball at the right moment and using the correct part of your forehead to hit the ball.

Watch the flight path of the ball, and as it approaches make sure your neck muscles are stiff. Use your arms to both lift and balance you, as you jump into the air to meet the ball. Arch your back and bend your knees, to give you additional lift as you jump.

If you use the top of your head the ball could go in any direction. If it hits the bridge of your nose you will not need me to tell you how much it will hurt!

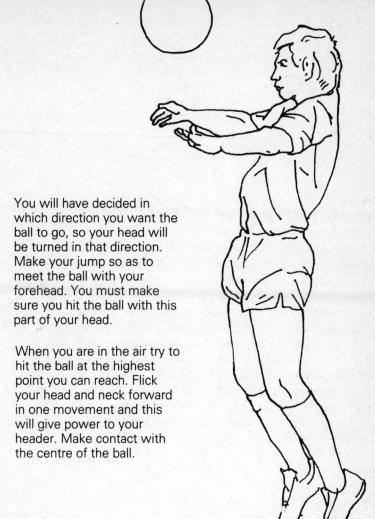

You will have decided in which direction you want the ball to go, so your head will be turned in that direction. Make your jump so as to meet the ball with your forehead. You must make sure you hit the ball with this part of your head.

When you are in the air try to hit the ball at the highest point you can reach. Flick your head and neck forward in one movement and this will give power to your header. Make contact with the centre of the ball.

One final note. As you come down from your jump, concentrate on landing safely on your feet.

Do not be afraid of heading the ball. Learn how to do it properly and you will gain confidence in your ability.

FAULT-FINDER

Remember that you must make your head hit the ball rather than the ball hitting your head. There is a big difference.

In today's game there are a lot of players who have exceptional ability at heading the ball. It is not a skill used in any particular position, but can be a great asset to both strikers and defenders. Two strikers who spring to mind as being exceptional in the air are Mick Harford, and Graeme Sharp. Not only do these two score goals with their heads they also create opportunities for their team-mates from mid-air.

Defenders do tend, however, to have a little more power behind their head shots than the average striker. Two examples of defenders with above average heading ability, Dave Watson and Terry Butcher.

A player with good heading skills is always an asset to the team, whether he is a defender or a forward. He will be in demand to take corners and free kicks. Defensive players will be trying to head the ball up and out of the area while attacking players will be trying to head the ball down into goal.

Tackling

Tackling is the use of the feet to take the ball away from an opponent. It is an important skill for all players to learn. Some players think that only defensive team members need know how to tackle. This is not the case. Every player, including the goalkeeper should know how to make a clean tackle. Here are a few points to keep in mind, when preparing to make a tackle.

LAW-BREAKER
*The referee will award a DIRECT FREE-KICK against a you if you deliberately, kick or try to kick an opponent; trip an opponent; jump at an opponent; charge an opponent in a violent or dangerous way or from behind unless he is obstructing you; strike or try to strike an opponent or spit at him; hold an opponent; push an opponent; or handle the ball, (This does not apply to the goalkeeper within his own penalty-area).
If any of the offences is committed within the penalty-area. the referee will award a PENALTY-KICK.*

1. Concentrate on the ball, not on the opponent with the ball. You must keep your eyes on the ball at all times.

2. You should use the side of your foot to make contact with the ball. Avoid kicking your opponent's leg as this is foul play and you will be penalised by the referee.

3. The weight of your body should be behind you during the tackle. Your aim is to put your whole leg and entire body weight into the tackle at the same time. If you just stick your leg in on a tackle without having your body weight behind you, someone could get hurt – and it could be you. If you are half-hearted about your challenge and your opponent is going in with the full force of his body weight, you will certainly be knocked out of the way.

The sliding tackle is the 'last resort' tackle. Take the ball cleanly, keeping your foot down to avoid tripping your opponent.

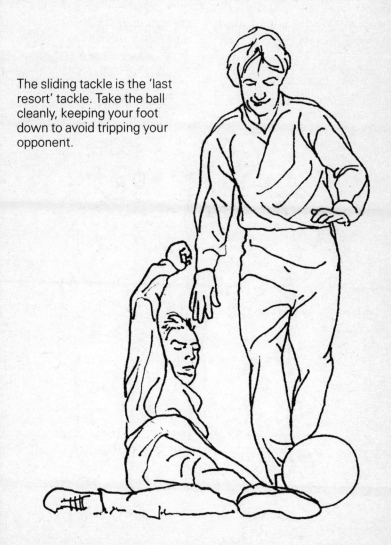

Shoulder charge

Another common tackle is the shoulder charge. With this tackle you must manouevre yourself into position, running alongside the player with the ball.

You should be in a slightly crouching position, as you come shoulder to shoulder with your opponent. When you make contact with him, shift your entire weight into the shoulder you are going to use and back this up with the supporting leg to give you balance. Using the side of your foot, as if you were going to kick the ball, apply pressure to the ball to force your opponent to lose possession.

This shoulder-to-shoulder charge is legal in football if executed properly. The purpose of this challenge is to unbalance your opponent to enable you to get the ball while running. You must not use your elbows, hands, or hips in a shoulder charge. You must use only your shoulders. You may only use the shoulder charge when the ball is within playing distance of the player you are challenging, ie. you must not shoulder charge an opponent when the ball is at the other side of the field.

If you can remember to make contact with the ball and use the weight of your body in the tackle it can be an important and effective skill to enable you to win the ball for your side.

LAW-BREAKER
The Referee will award an INDIRECT FREE-KICK against your side if you indulge in tactics which, in the opinion or the Referee, are designed merely to hold up the game and thus waste time and so give an unfair advantage to your own team.

THE REFEREE'S DECISION
He will award a PENALTY-KICK, if the ball is in play, wherever it is at the time, if any of the following offences occurs in the penalty-area. Playing dangerously, e.g. attempting to kick the ball while held by the goalkeeper; Charging fairly, ie. with the shoulder, when the ball is not within playing distance of the players concerned and they are definitely not trying to play it; When not playing the ball, intentionally obstructing an opponent; Charging the goalkeeper except when he:
(a) is holding the ball; (b) is obstructing an opponent; (c) has passed outside his goal-area.

Shielding the ball

It is essential for players who play up front to learn how to shield the ball effectively. To enable you to shield the ball to your best advantage, you must get the whole of your body between the ball and your opponent.

It is not, however, within the laws of the game to actually hold your opponent or pull his clothing. This would constitute a foul, so you would lose the advantage that you gained from keeping him off the ball.

A good example of a player who really excelled at shielding the ball is Kenny Dalglish. Peter Beardsley and John Barnes are also masters of this skill.

Many continental teams consider shielding to be an important factor in their game and spend time perfecting their players' skills.

Shielding the ball can be an asset to your game when for example, a player is up in his opposing half and a team-mate passes the ball to him from the defending half. If the forward player is good at shielding the ball, he could hold off any challenger until his team-mates have got up the field to support him.

You should have either your elbows sticking out at the sides of your body, or your arms stretched out at your sides. This makes your body area greater, as your opponent must go round your outstretched arms. He cannot run through you!

You must know where your opponent is behind you even to the point of leaning back slightly on to him.

Your arms and hips are your greatest assets when shielding the ball as these parts increase the overall area of your body and the greater your body area the more difficult it is for your opponent to get round you. It is also advisable to keep the ball on the foot furthest away from your opponent, once again putting more distance between him and the ball.

Goalkeeping

To describe the full technical role of the goalkeeper would require a book all of its own.

However, here is a brief description of the basics. The technique of stopping the ball is just the same as for any outfield player, with the obvious advantage that the keeper can use his hands as an additional means of controlling the ball. In general, the following principles apply to goalkeeping:

FAULT-FINDER

Most mistakes made by goalkeepers are caused when they take their eyes off the ball. They may be looking to make a quick kick or throw-out, or they may be looking to see if an opponent is coming in direct challenge. These mistakes can be fatal and therefore it is vital for a goalkeeper to work on his concentration and avoid such disasters.

1. Your body should be behind the ball whenever possible.

2. You should use two hands to make a save or catch when you have the opportunity.

3. As you catch the ball, allow your body to relax and your arms to withdraw backwards to absorb the impact of the shot.
4. Always concentrate on the flight path of the ball. Keep your eyes on the ball at all times.

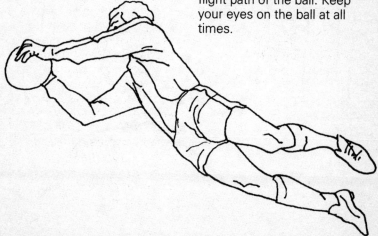

Catching the ball cleanly and positively is most important. Having caught and controlled the ball, the goalkeeper is in a position of total authority in the game.

Always remember to keep your hands in a 'W' shape, with palms facing outwards and thumbs together. This gives an additional safety net by stopping the ball from going straight through.

Goalkeepers are required to catch the ball at all heights, from above his head to sideways and at ground level. The ball should be pulled into the stomach after a save as quickly as possible, to use your body as protection from an immediate challenge.

For a ground save, the goalkeeper should put the largest possible area of himself behind the ball. This is usually best achieved by going down on one knee, making sure there are no gaps between your legs.

Your arms should be at shoulder-width, with hands close together at ground level with your palms upturned. This gives a channel into the stomach to guide the ball upwards. When you are kneeling, keep your eyes on a level with the flight path of the ball.

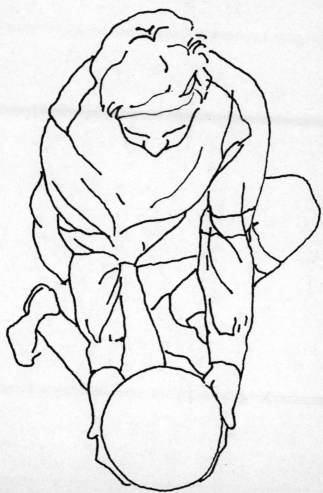

If the ball is above ground-level and below chest-height, you can bend forward from the waist, arms hanging down with palms turned outwards again to form a channel for the ball. Your legs must be closed together as back-up to stop the ball dribbling through.

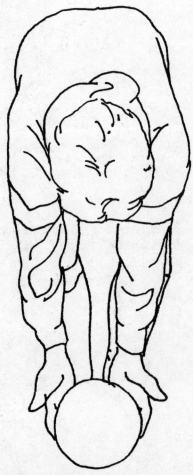

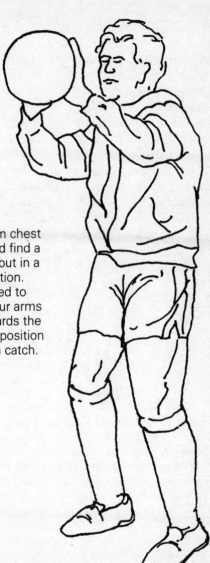

Balls approaching from chest height or above should find a goalkeeper standing, but in a slightly crouched position. You should be prepared to jump if necessary. Your arms should be raised towards the ball, hands in the 'W' position ready to make a clean catch.

Good goalkeepers can catch and hold the ball in almost any circumstances. Any inclination to push the ball and knock it down must be avoided. If you are stretched to catch it cleanly, make sure that you get the ball away from the danger zone of the penalty area. Tipping the ball over the bar or punching it around the uprights may look very spectacular, but unless saves like this are strictly necessary they will not earn you the respect of your fellow players. Their hearts will be in their mouths until the ball is safely under control. An expert catcher will make everyone feel more confident and secure.

Whenever possible a goalkeeper should move towards a shot or cross to deal with it. The obvious advantage is that he will be there sooner and will already be into his stride, enabling him to jump higher and off his best lifting foot if required. A goalkeeper needs to be on the move at all times if there is any likelihood of his having to go for a ball. If you are already moving you will be much sharper at your run, jump or spring, than if you have to make a standing start.

LAW-BREAKER

The referee will award an INDIRECT FREE-KICK against you if, (within your own penalty-area) from the moment you take control of the ball with your hands, you take more than four steps in any direction whilst holding, bouncing or throwing the ball in the air and catching it again, without releasing it into play, or, having released the ball into play before, during or after the four steps, touch it again with your hands, before it has been touched or played by another player of the same team outside of the penalty-area or by a player of the opposing team either inside or outside of the penalty-area.

Obviously there are times when it is vital and necessary to punch the ball or tip it over the crossbar and there are techniques for both possibilities.

When punching, some keepers prefer to use both fists as this gives a larger, flatter surface. However I prefer the teaching of one-handed punching. If the keeper has to jump he can obtain more lift from using his other arm to help raise him in the air. It is usually a matter of personal preference which method the keeper uses.

Of course there will be instances when only one hand can be used and most keepers use a natural overarm swing to hit the ball in the required direction. There are a number of methods for tipping the ball up and over. Try to adopt one which gets as much of your fingers and part of the palm of your hand on the ball as possible as this will give you greater accuracy and control.

Angles

If you can master angles it will be a great addition to your goalkeeping skills. The aim is to make the target area as small as possible. If you stand on the line in the middle of your goal, the opposition has a large area to shoot at. Therefore you must come out from the line and narrow the angle of the target area. This is best described in the diagram below.

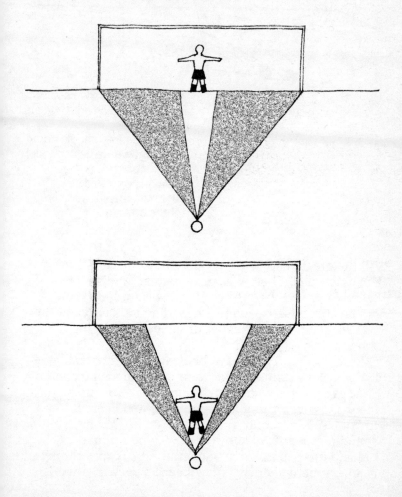

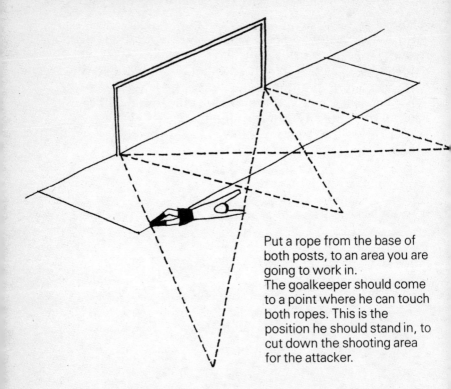

Put a rope from the base of both posts, to an area you are going to work in.
The goalkeeper should come to a point where he can touch both ropes. This is the position he should stand in, to cut down the shooting area for the attacker.

All the great keepers of our time have mastered the art of angle skills. There was once a great English keeper called Harry Hibbs. Although he was under 6 ft tall, his positional sense made everything look easy and he was nicknamed 'the keeper of the ever-changing triangle'.

In my opinion Bruce Grobbelaar is the most talented keeper playing in today's game. Not only is he good at crosses, his angles and positional sense are amazing. He makes everything look effortless and easy. If I had to criticise him for anything it would be that he sometimes wants to show how well he can play outside the penalty area. Generally speaking I think he is an excellent keeper. I once heard a keeper, a world class 'goalie' himself, describe Grobbelaar by saying: "If you could roll Ray Clemence and Peter Shilton into one then you would have Bruce Grobbelaar."

Young keepers should watch carefully how good professionals handle situations. They do not always make spectacular saves. They learn that they do not need to dive about or make things look more difficult than they really are. They know how to diffuse difficult situations, by being aware when to come and take crosses. They make themselves appear 'big' to the opposing forwards, making the target look 'small'. All the great keepers in the history of the game, men like Swift, Yashin, Jennings, Shilton, Southall and Grobbelaar have obviously been in control of the penalty area. They also seem to have great charisma and a tremendous rapport with the spectators.

How many times have you watched a game or read a report which says the keeper had nothing to do for the whole game or never made a worthwhile save? Just consider why it seems as if he has had nothing to do. It is because in many cases he has done nothing spectacular and made all his saves look easy. His distribution will also have been just as it should be, finding its intended targets throughout the game. He will have realised when to set up attacks for his team-mates with a quick throw or kick. The goalkeeper has worked so hard on his game and on improving his own individual techniques and awareness, that during the match, everything has become second nature. Everything he does looks easy because he has made it that way. As I have stressed in other chapters practice is what improves skills, no matter how difficult they may appear at first. There is no substitute for hard work. A clean sheet for a keeper is as much a prize as a goal for a striker. The more clean sheets, the better his reputation.

I always maintain that you only appreciate a top-class keeper when you do not have one!

Systems and Tactics

A system of play is a recognisable pattern with which each and every player becomes familiar. A manager and coach will choose a system as part of their team tactics. It should make the best use of available players, allow flexibility for the talent of individuals and ensure that they work within a team framework which will achieve the desired result.

These systems might be 4-4-2, 4-3-3 etc (see chart)

One of the questions asked most often is: Should the players fit the system or the system fit the players?

I think it is important to remember that it is not systems alone which win matches it is the players within the system who get results.

Otherwise, it would follow that for example, in a game in which both teams are playing 4-4-2, the two will cancel each other out. Evidently that does not happen because of the individuals within the framework, who produce the required skill or their own little bit of magic to win the game. Successful teams like Liverpool and Everton choose their formation and indeed their game tactics as a whole, to make the best possible use of their players. Although it hurts me to admit it as an attacking footballer, it is defence that is the first area of tactics that needs to be confronted in any side. Once that has been sorted out the manager has something to build on. In Britain zonal defence is most commonly adopted and the current Liverpool team are the best example of its success. They have full backs who can see what is happening and cover, while the centre halves can play the dual role of attacking the ball or covering for the man doing so, so zonal defence works for Liverpool.

Whilst Queen's Park Rangers are an outstanding exception in the league because they play man-to-man marking. It works for QPR because they have quick defenders who can read the game and play with skill. (Man-to-man marking and zonal defence will be described fully later.) This simply illustrates the point that no system or tactics will work unless they take into account the ability of the players and changes in the game. Zonal-defence for example started in the 1960's. It was one of the things to come out of the F.A. think-tank of the time.

In the '50's defenders were mostly big, physical players who were not expected to show a great deal of skill. They were expected to stop the ball. Zonal defence changed the role of the defender. He was now expected to be quicker, fitter and more skilful, more of an all round player. He needed to play a more aggressive game if he was to get possession of the ball and bring it into play for the rest of the team. Developments in formation came out of his new role. Of course there are many sides still, who play with five-man defences, consisting of three centre backs and two full backs. But this is often only a case of safety in numbers and can be exposed as such when they try to change to a four-man line-up and finish short of knowhow.

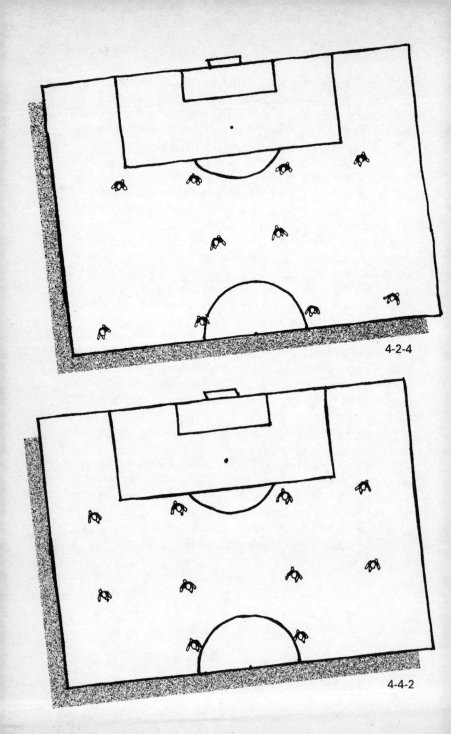

4-2-4

4-4-2

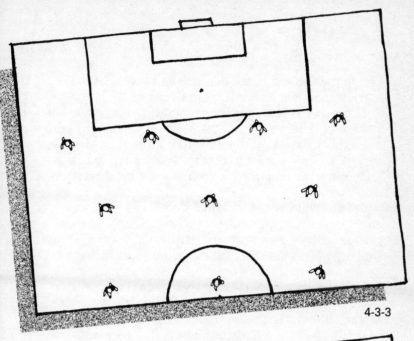

4-3-3

4-3-3

Defence

I have mentioned zonal defence and man-to-man marking. So lets look at this in detail.

There are differing opinions about which is the best system of defence. Many people believe that the game should be played on the man-to-man basis, using a sweeper. This is adopted by most continental teams. Each player is responsible for marking his direct opponent.

Others will insist that zonal defence is best, in which each player is responsible for a specific area of the pitch and only picks up and marks players who enter that area. This system is adopted by most British teams.

It should be made clear at this stage that in either man-to-man or zonal defence systems when a team attacks, the defence reinforce their forwards in search of goals and when a team defends, the forwards fall back and fill gaps in front of their defenders to avoid conceding any goals.

Man-to-man

There are arguments for and against both systems. In a rigid man-to-man system each player should be responsible for his direct opponent for the entire match. However this can be a totally unrealistic approach for the whole 90 minutes. If an opponent breaks free with the ball he should, in theory, be able to exploit any advantage he has gained and should be able to run through the opposing defence unchallenged.

However, what happens in reality is that the defending team withdraws and the sweeper confronts the player who has broken free, coming towards him

MAN-TO-MAN MARKING
Each defender covers a specific attacker.
The sweeper picks up anyone breaking through.

with the ball. If the sweeper cannot counteract the
situation then defenders move across to defuse the
immediate danger, thus leaving an attacker free in the
least dangerous position. Every player guards or marks
a specific opponent in a man-to-man system. The main
point to remember with this type of defence is that you
must never leave your man. He is your responsibility
and it is your job to slow down his movement. You
must prevent him from getting into a position to take a
shot at goal or even from making a pass to someone

who is in a goal scoring position. It is no good expecting someone else to pick up your player because each man has his own responsibilities.

You do not have to be a university graduate or great thinker on the game to follow this kind of tactic. In fact as long as you are suitably prepared and defensively-minded and prepared to stick at the job it can be done. You can even get by in this role if you are a less-skilled player as long as you have a mobility about your game and a willingness to put it to use and sacrifice yourself for the team.

LAW-BREAKER

Be very careful when moving into position or you could be OFF-SIDE, if you are nearer to your opponent's goal-line than the ball unless, you are in your own half of the field of play, or there are at least two of your opponents nearer their own goal-line than you are.

THE REFEREE'S DECISION

A player will only be declared off-side and penalised for being in an off-side position, if, at the moment the ball touches, or is played by, one of his team, he is, interfering with play or with an opponent, or seeking to gain an advantage by being in that position.

Incidentally you won't be declared off-side merely because you are in an off-side position, or if you receive the ball, direct, from a goal-kick, a corner-kick, a throw-in, or when it has been dropped by the Referee.

If a player is declared off-side, the referee will award an INDIRECT FREE-KICK.

Zonal Defence

In zonal defence, each player guards or covers a specific area or zone of the field. The field is divided up into particular sections and each player is assigned to one of these to cover during the game. If an opposing player comes into this zone you are responsible for slowing down his progress and counteracting any productive play by him. Again there are advantages and disadvantages with this system.

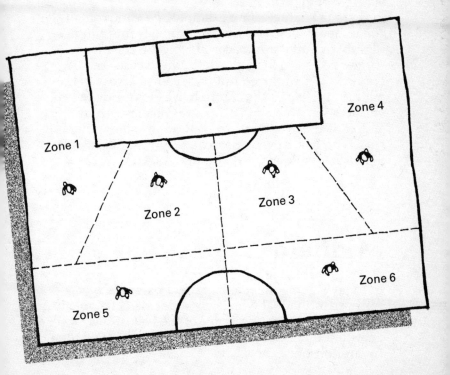

ZONAL DEFENCE
Each defender is responsible for a specific area

An advantage is that you are not chasing a player all over the field as with the man-to-man system. The disadvantage is that zonal defence requires a lot more thought and constant talking between players.

There must be constant communication. If a player with the ball leaves your area and moves to another zone, you must let your other defenders know he is coming his way. 'Pick him up' is the common cry.

There is one area in which zonal defence cannot be used and that is the penalty area. Whenever an opposing player has the ball in your penalty box you must switch to a man-to-man defence. This could arise from a set-piece, corner kick or just in general play. An opposing player must never be left unguarded in the penalty area, otherwise he will be completely free to take a shot at goal.

There is an interesting example of a variation on this zonal theme in Scotland where some teams adopt a slightly different approach, playing 4-3-3 with one winger added to their attack. In these cases the opposite, unemployed full-back comes across to the middle and leaves the centre-halves to decide which will act as a sweeper. The main problem with this system is that the midfield man on the side of the full-back who has moved has extra responsibilities with defensive work and can lose his attacking threat.

Midfield

In today's game the ideal midfield player is an all-purpose individual who is good defensively, able to tackle and a good distributor of the ball. If he can score goals too that is a bonus. Every team is looking for a Bryan Robson.

It used to be the case that the midfield man was skilful, passed to attacking team-mates and made the side tick. When I was younger, the aim was to play through the middle and pick out the wingers to spring attacks. It was the pivot of the teams' play when there was more time to use your skills.

Fitness

But above all remember you need to work at your fitness to do well in the midfield. The level of skill is nowhere near as high as it was 10 years ago and a fit lad will get by where he would have been rejected previously. There is so much more emphasis on the competitive edge.

THE REFEREE'S DECISION

It's a goal when the whole of the ball has passed over the goal-line, between the goal-posts and under the cross-bar, provided it has not been thrown, carried or intentionally taken by hand or arm, by a player of the attacking side, except in the case of a goalkeeper, who is within his penalty area. The team which scores the greater number of goals during a game is the winner, if no goals, or an equal number of goals are scored, the game shall be termed a "draw".

THE REFEREE'S DECISION
*After a goal has been
scored, the game is
restarted with a place-kick,
taken by a player of the
team losing the goal.*

Attack

It is not absolutely vital to have natural ability to beat
opponents with blinding skill, if you want to become a
famous striker. If you have pace in today's game you
can become a top-class striker. I can think of many
players rated in the world class who have phenomenal
pace and average ability. There are also those with
superb ability and little pace. And then there are the
likes of Diego Maraddona who have both and make
millions of pounds as a result.

Gary Lineker is a perfect example of someone with
outstanding pace, but no great technical ability. Kenny
Dalglish has fantastic skill, but was not the greatest
runner ever seen. Jock Stein always said that the one
thing he lacked was that extra yard of pace, but in no
way did this hamper him. When I played with Kenny
at Celtic and something happened in the opposition's
half he was the first one on to it, ahead of the
defenders by two or three yards. He knew what was
going on because he was so alert to all openings. He
would never win the 100 yards dash, but in terms of
speed of thought he was way ahead of anyone else.
That is a talent you must be born with. Kenny Dalglish
had a great appetite for the game and the desire to be a
winner. He just loved playing. One of his biggest –
and most under-estimated qualities – was his courage.

He was always there to be found in the box, no matter
what was going on around or how hard the men
around him were. In terms of ability to turn his man
and create an opening, he is the best that Britain has
ever seen or produced. I can only think of Nigel
Clough of Nottingham Forest and Mark Hughes
in today's game who have a similar style to Kenny
Dalglish. Again, critics say they lack a yard of pace.

Striker
When you are young, the main thing you must be to
become a striker, is brave about scoring goals. You
must be single-minded about it. You have got to think
that any ball coming your way will become a shot and
hit that target. You must channel your mind in that
one direction, even to the point of being selfish. All
good strikers only think about scoring goals – and the
chances that could have come their way and what they
will do the next time.

A striker builds his reputation on the number of
strikes on goal that he can manage during a game.
There is no point in being a striker and never getting a
shot. You must always aim for the target, even a mis-
hit shot can make the keeper move for a save and that
can lead to something, either a mistake or a deflection.
A cracking shot over the bar is just a cracking shot over
the bar.

Nowadays you can have a good finisher whose
general play is diabolical. You have others who run
about and help the team. Peter Withe is a good
example of a target man who makes others play. He
encourages others into the play.

Wingers
Wingers of today are asked to play a midfield role
more than ever. As a result you need pace to be a
winger and make the transition from midfielder into
winger in the same game on a regular basis. However,

you still have to have wide men, because the game is so compact that there must be an outlet. If you cannot find a team-mate close by from defence, then you want to find someone away from the heart of the battle – and that is the winger. The widest part of the pitch is the touchline and that is where to aim, when you are hemmed in at the back and the central midfield is a mass of bodies.

Franz Carr is the one to study to see how this can operate perfectly and turn defence into attack. His phenomenal pace causes problems, but it is part of a counter-attacking style, where the midfield deliberately time their pass to spring him from midfield and catch the opposition at their weakest.

Midfield

Alan Hudson, once of Chelsea and England, was the best example I can think of, where skill predominated over more workmanlike qualities, Glen Hoddle is another. Players like that could adapt to play anywhere. But today, whatever their ability, they also need a much higher level of fitness.

The modern demands make the midfield man a marked man. When I was younger I would be marked in seven games out of ten. Sometimes the marker would stay with me for every second, sometimes just when I was in an attacking position. Today many midfielders have a constant shadow with the stress coming from manager and coaches towards tight marking.

The normal midfield comprises two men in the middle and two wide, who can act as full backs and wingers during the game. The men in the middle have to be able to get up and back.

But one thing that does not change for the midfielder is his level of awareness of the overall play. You have to be more alert to the game in this area than any other. This position is still the brains of the team.

They must think themselves. But they must grasp

the basic system and make it work for their team-mates as well.

Passing ability
Passing ability is the first quality I would look for in a midfielder. If you ask a group of youngsters to pick out the midfielder in their group, it will be the best passer and I firmly believe that youngsters can be the best 'coaches' when it comes to spotting one another's respective strengths.

Awareness
Awareness comes from experience and of course natural ability. When you have possession you have to know what alternatives there are for your attack, you have to play and forward plan. When you lose the ball you have to think of how to stop the opposition playing.

You improve awareness by thinking over your last game – even the nightmares! Jock Stein always preached to me, that no matter how badly I had played for 89 minutes there was always the ninetieth one to score a goal and get the headlines.

I lost count of the number of times I did that, sneaking a goal after having a game I would rather forget. This is the way all forwards and midfielders have to think. Never give up, but always remember what you were doing wrong and how to put it right the next time.

Look at Peter Reid of Everton and England if you want to see how midfielders can get the ball and be efficient on it. He is never afraid of the ball and that is the only way to be. You cannot have a good or bad game if you do not get a kick. You just have not played.

Reid is a great example of a player who helps others make runs. His distribution of the ball is excellent and his keeness to get into areas where he and his team-mates can hurt the opposition is outstanding.

Nowadays, with virtually every team pushing on to the halfway line to defend, it denies the midfield man space to operate. It is harder than ever to be a Peter Reid because of that, but there are ways of living in that stifling atmosphere.

Pressing football is the new theory and it is interesting to note that the Dutch who invented it also had a special way of preparing their stars to cope with the problems it caused, ie. lack of space and rushing the thought process. Remember that they managed to produce the like of Johann Cruyff and Ruud Gullit.

The Dutch in the 60's and 70's decided that all their young players should be made to play in more than one position which would enable them to become good players in at least two roles. Until the age of 14 they are not allowed to specialize in one position. It helps to produce players who are capable of playing several roles and can operate safely and think when they are caught out of their normal position. This often happens when the play is condensed by the opposition.

I would suggest it is worthwhile for every youngster to try and master the art of playing in more than one position and so get a better idea of the demands of the game.

This variety is good for any young player because then they can see what sort of passes are better to receive and to give.

Systems and Tactics Abroad

I would like to give some personal examples of my experiences of different systems and tactics from playing in Portugal.

It was an excellent opportunity to see first-hand how different countries differ in their ideas on how the game should be played. The biggest difference I noticed was that the average Portuguese player had far more ability than the average British player. This came as something of a shock to me, as I did not expect this to be the case at all.

It is strange when you consider the level of skill there is among their players. I never lagged behind in terms of skill at the clubs I played for in Britain. But I could not match any of these guys.

The Portuguese depend upon their skill when attacking, whereas British teams have a much more direct approach, using power and speed. Most Portuguese and continental teams like to defend in numbers and get as many players as possible around the ball. They also play a man-to-man system, with the sweeper clearing up behind the defence. The sweeper is the most important member of a team playing with this system. He is responsible for and covers for any mistakes made by the team. He also instigates and orchestrates all attacks from the back.

They concentrate strongly on their passing. They are very negative in their attitude and outlook towards scoring goals, preferring not to concede any instead. They make lots of passes in their own half of the field, just content to keep possession of the ball. This is to attract the opposition into their half. Then, at the stage when they have drawn enough opponents into their half, they will try to play a long ball forward and catch the opposition out. This type of game is very much a cat and mouse approach and their entire game is based on this counter-attack policy.

This is entirely different to the British way of thinking. There are various reasons for this. I believe the main one is the Portuguese climate. Sometimes they play in temperatures of up to 90 degrees. To play a fast and typically British type of game would be almost impossible. Instead their game is played at a much slower pace and with a more cautious outlook. The emphasis is on passing and as little running around in the heat as possible.

Their belief is that if they have possession of the ball then the opposition cannot score any goals. In theory this is absolutely correct. When a team plays away from home, the onus is always on the home team to score goals and entertain the home fans.

I recall playing with five defenders, four midfield men and one striker. If we were winning by one goal away from home with 15 minutes to go in the game, it was common for the coaches to take off a midfield player and put on another – sixth – defender. The coaches are only interested in the results. This is the case the world over, of course. But this is an extreme outlook.

In Britain, teams try to play whether they are at home or away. It is a very true, if cliched, saying that football is a funny old game. In Britain, there are more and more continental games on the television and the move of top British stars abroad has heightened interest in other types of football. It is common for people to say it would be great to see that type of football in Britain, but I know without fear of contradiction that all around Europe fans want to see British games being played and British Cup Finals are beamed live around the globe. I also know of coaches abroad who refer to the British style of play as being the best and most exciting.

I think it is best left to each individual to decide which, in their opinion, is the right way to play although, I must say that it is a good idea to try and look further than their own doorstep to see the alternatives and perhaps learn from other styles. The Germans have a lot to offer for example they have welded continental ball skills with British aggression, making them the most successful country at club and international level in recent years.

Each nation finds its own kind of football, depending on a collection of circumstances, and it is up to the next generation to shape their national game in their own way. Every type of football has its good and bad points and everyone can be changed and improved in some way. That is the excitement and interest in this great game.

Match Rules

The Ball

The ball used for soccer is spherical; the outer casing is made of leather or other approved materials. The main consideration is that there is nothing used in the construction which might prove dangerous to the players. The circumference of the ball should be not more than 28 in. and not less than 27 in. The weight of the ball at the start of the game should not be more than 16 oz. nor less than 14 oz. The pressure should be equal to 0.6-1.1 atmosphere (equals 600-1100 gr/cm2) at sea level. The ball shall not be changed during the game unless authorised by the Referee. Schoolboys and youngsters may use a smaller ball.

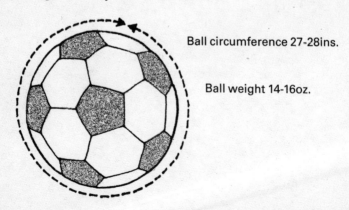

Ball circumference 27-28ins.

Ball weight 14-16oz.

The teams

A match is played by two teams, each consisting of not more than eleven players, one of whom is the goalkeeper.

Substitutes may be used in any match played under the rules of an official competition at FIFA, Confederation or National Association level, subject to the conditions stated in the rulebook.

Any of the other players may change places with the goalkeeper, provided that the referee is informed before the change is made, and provided also that the change is made during a stoppage in the game.

When a goalkeeper or any other player is to be replaced by a substitute, the referee must be informed of the proposed substitution, before it is made.

The substitute can't enter the field of play until the player he is replacing has left, and then only after having received a signal from the referee.

He must come on during a stoppage in the game, and at the half-way line. A player who has been replaced can't take any further part in the game. A substitute is subject to the authority and jurisdiction of the referee whether called upon to play or not.

The substitution is complete when the substitute enters the field of play, from which moment he becomes a player and the player who he is replacing ceases to be a player.

Length of game

The duration of the game is of two equal periods of 45 minutes, unless otherwise mutually agreed upon, subject to the following: Allowance will be made in either period for all time lost through substitution, the transport from the field of injured players, time-wasting or other causes, the amount of which is at the discretion of the Referee: The time will also be extended to allow a penalty kick to be taken at or after the expiration of the normal period in either half.

At half-time the interval won't exceed five minutes except by consent of the Referee.

The referee
A referee is appointed to officiate in each game. His authority and the exercise of the powers granted to him begins as soon as he comes on to the pitch and extends to those times when play is suspended.

His decision on points of fact connected with the play is final, so far as the result of the game is concerned.

He enforces the Laws and uses his discretion in punishment, keeps a record of the game; acts as timekeeper and allows the full or agreed time, adding on injury and stoppage time.

He can stop the game for any infringement of the Laws and suspend or terminate the game because of the weather or bad behaviour from the spectators.

The linesmen
The two appointed linesmen help the referee by signalling :-
1. When the ball is out of play;
2. Corner-kick, goal-kick or throw-in;
3. When a substitution is needed.

The Start of Play

At the beginning of the game, choice of ends and the kick-off is decided by the toss of a coin. The team winning the toss has the option of choice of ends or the kick-off.

The referee gives the signal to start the game. A player takes a place-kick (ie. a kick at the ball while it is stationary on the ground in the centre of the field of play) into his opponents' half. All the players in the opposing team must stay 10 yards from the ball until it is kicked-off.

The kicker musn't play the ball a second time until it has been touched or played by another player.

If he does, an indirect free-kick is taken by a player of the opposing team from the place where the infringement occurred. You can't score direct from a kick-off.

Half-time
After half-time the game restarts and the teams change ends. The kick-off is taken by a player of the opposite team to that of the player who started the game.

Any infringement of kick-off rules will mean the kick-off is retaken, except in the case of the kicker playing the ball again before it has been touched or played by another player.

Re-starting the game
When re-starting the game after any other temporary suspension of play, unless the ball has gone over the touch or goal-lines the referee will drop the ball at the point when it was last in play. It isn't in play until it has touched the ground. If the play was suspended in the goal-area, he will drop it on the part of the goal-area line, which runs parallel to the goal-line, at the

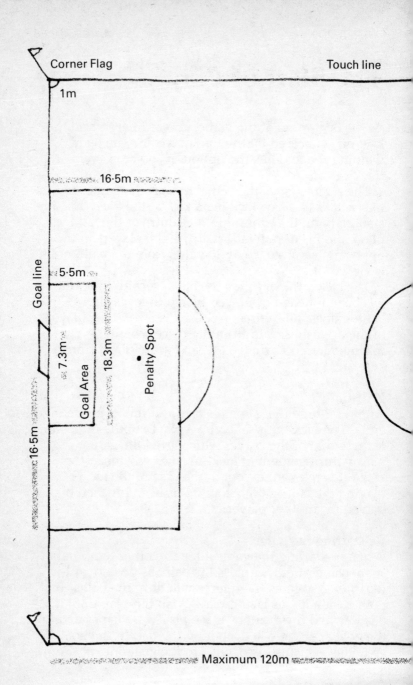

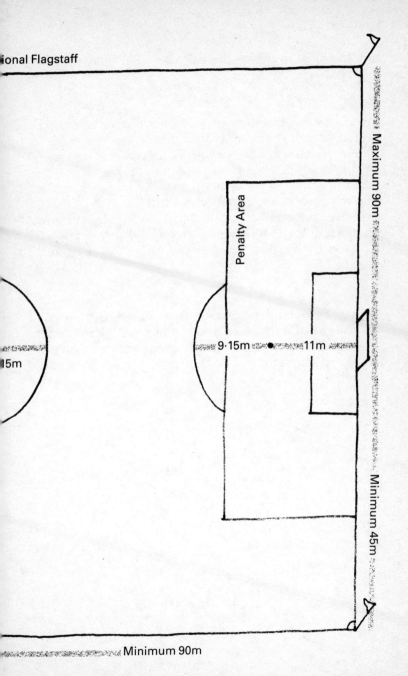

point nearest to where the ball was when play was
stopped.

Free-kicks
Free-kicks can be either direct from which a goal can be
scored or indirect from which a goal can't be scored.
The free-kick will be taken by the opposing side from
the place where the offence occurred. If the offences
occur in the opponents' goal-area, the free-kick can be
taken from a point anywhere within that half of the
goal-area. Opposing players must stand 9.15m or more
away from the ball while the free-kick is being taken.
You can't score directly against your own side from a
free-kick.

Penalty-kicks
A penalty-kick must be taken from the penalty-mark
and all the other players and the opposing goalkeeper,
must stand outside the penalty-area. The opposing
goalkeeper must stand (without moving his feet) on

his own goal-line, between the goal-posts, until the ball is kicked. The player taking the kick must kick the ball forward; he must not play the ball a second time until it has been touched or played by another player. The ball shall be deemed in play directly it is kicked, ie. travelled the distance of its circumference. A goal may be scored directly from a penalty-kick. When a penalty-kick is being taken during the normal course of play, or when time has been extended at half-time or full-time to allow a penalty-kick to be taken or retaken, a goal shall not be nullified if, before passing between the posts and under the cross-bar, the ball touches either or both of the goal-posts, or the cross-bar, or the goalkeeper, or any combination of these agencies, providing that no other infringement has occurred.

Goal-kick
When the whole of the ball passes over the goal-line excluding that portion between the goal-posts, either in the air or on the ground having last been played by one of the attacking team, it must be kicked directly into play beyond the penalty-area from a point within that half of the goal-area nearest to where it crossed the line, by a player of the defending team. A goalkeeper must not receive the ball into his hands from a goal-kick in order that he may kick it into play. If the ball is not kicked beyond the penalty-area, ie. directly into play, the kick shall be retaken. The kicker must not play the ball a second time until it has touched or been played by another player. A goal cannot be scored direct from such a kick. Players of the team opposing that of the player taking the goal-kick must remain outside the penalty-area until the ball as been kicked out of the penalty-area.

Corner-kick

When the whole of the ball passes over the goal-line, excluding that portion between the goalposts, either in the air or on the ground, having last been played by one of the defending team, a member of the attacking team will take a corner-kick, ie. the whole of the ball will be placed within the quarter circle at the nearest corner flagpost, which must not be moved, and kicked from that position.

A goal may be scored direct from such a kick. Players of the team opposing that of the player taking the corner-kick must not approach within 10 yards of the ball until it is in play, ie. it has travelled the distance of its own circumference, nor must the kicker play the ball a second time until it has been touched or played by another player.

Throw-in

When the whole of the ball passes over a touchline, either on the ground or in the air, it must be thrown in from the point where it crossed the line, in any direction, by a player of the team opposite to that of the player who last touched it. The thrower at the moment of delivering the ball must face the field of play and part of each foot must be either on the touch-line or on the ground outside the touch-line. The thrower must use both hands and deliver the ball from behind and over his head. The ball is in play immediately it enters the field of play, but the thrower cannot again play the ball until it has been touched or played by another player. A goal may not be scored direct from a throw-in.

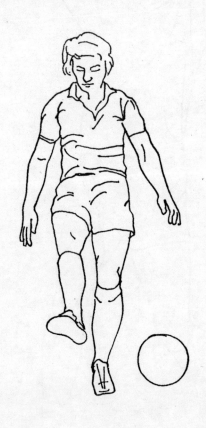